Dragons of Moon Tail Island

A Visit to Uncle Vesper

Written by Sam Gayton
Illustrated by Lisa Hunt

OXFORD
UNIVERSITY PRESS

Meet the characters ...
Ember and Nimbus are dragons from Moon Tail Island.
Nadia and Omar are friends with Ember and Nimbus. Humans can only be seen by dragons who believe in them.
Nini, the children's gran
?
a new dragon!

Ember and Nimbus were looping and swooping in the sky above Moon Tail Island.

The children held on tight as the two dragons raced each other from cloud to cloud. Nimbus soared to the **right** and Ember raced after him.

‘We won!’ yelled Omar, as Nimbus reached the next cloud.

‘Well done!’ Nadia called out. ‘We were *just* **behind** you!’

Omar and Nimbus are **in front of** Nadia and Ember. Is this correct?

Nimbus did a **half turn** and came back to Ember.

'We can't play in the sky all day,' said Nimbus.

Ember nodded. 'Yes, Uncle Vesper is expecting us.'

Which way do you face after completing a **half turn**?

Ember's Uncle Vesper had invited them to tea. Ember explained that her uncle liked to invent things and that he had a workshop near the forest.

'Can you remember how to get to Uncle Vesper's workshop?' said Nimbus.

‘From the top of Sharp Tooth Bay, fly a **quarter turn clockwise** to face the caves,’ said Ember. ‘Uncle Vesper’s workshop is **between** the caves and the volcano.’

‘OK, let’s get going!’ said Nimbus.

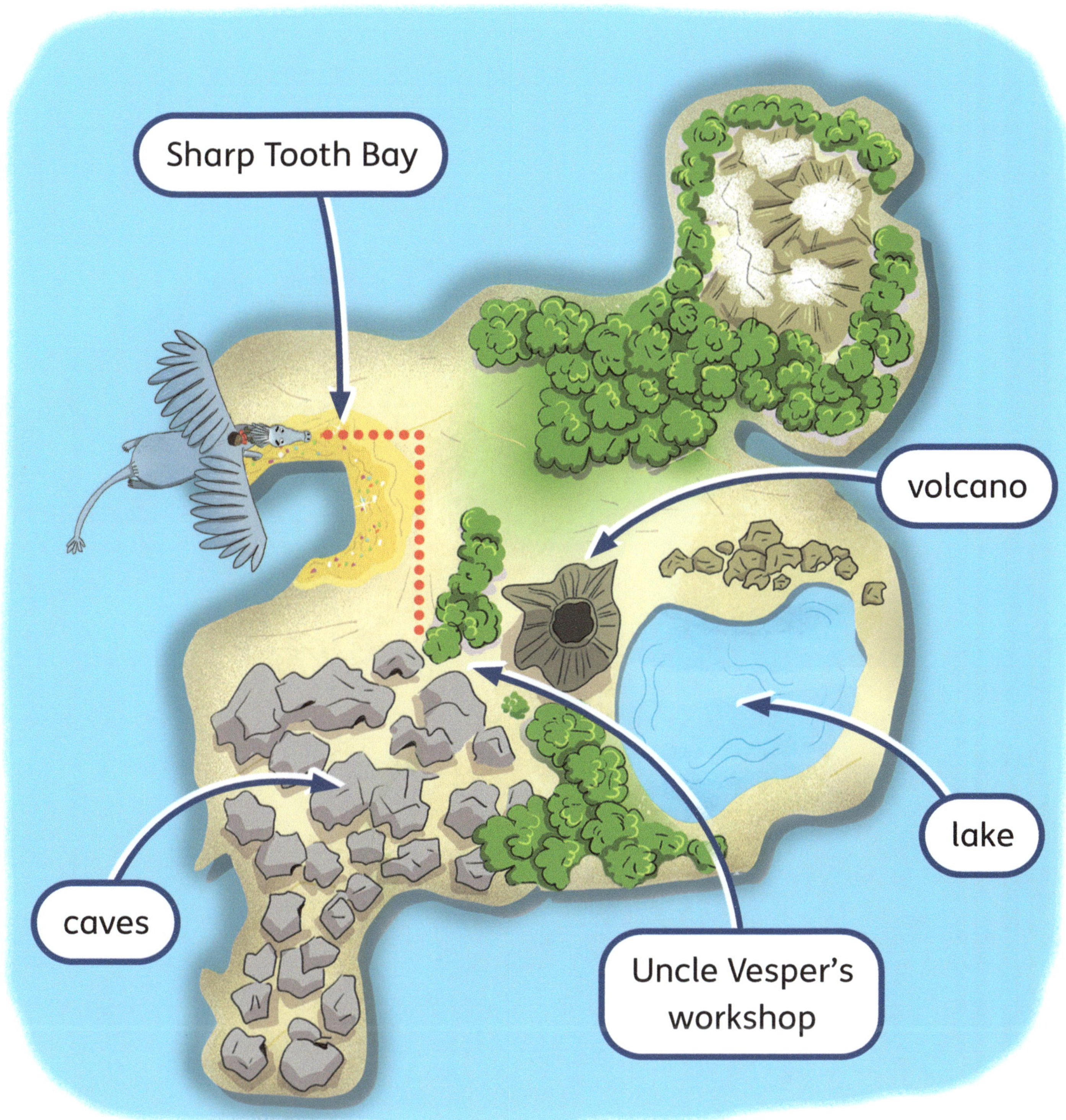

Look at the map. What is **to the right of** Uncle Vesper’s workshop?

Ember and Nadia raced ahead. They were first to reach Uncle Vesper's workshop. The workshop was built into a giant tree.

Suddenly, there was a loud noise, and smoke came out of the windows.

'Oh, crumbs!' said a surprised voice.

The dragons landed. ‘Uncle Vesper, are you OK?’ called Ember.

A gold and red dragon came outside. The end of his beard was sizzling.

‘Oh, yes, I’m fine!’ said Uncle Vesper quickly. He dunked his beard into a mug of tea.

Uncle Vesper put on his glasses. Then he looked from **left** to **right**.

'Goodness me,' he said to Ember. 'You've got two humans with you!'

Who is standing **to the left of** Uncle Vesper as you look at the page?

'You can see us?' said Nadia. 'How?'

'That's a long story,' said Uncle Vesper with a grin.

'And like all good stories, it has a surprise!' said a familiar voice **behind** him.

Nadia and Omar couldn't believe it. 'Nini!' they cried, rushing up to hug her.

'Vesper and I have been friends for a very long time,' explained Nini. 'We first met when I was around your age.'

'I suspected that you two had made some dragon friends of your own,' said Nini.

Nadia and Omar were amazed.

'This calls for a special tea party!' said Uncle Vesper. 'With cake … lots of cake! Follow me!'

Who is walking just **behind** Nini?

Uncle Vesper led them through his workshop. There were all sorts of inventions on the shelves.

They reached a big board with some paper on it. Uncle Vesper showed them a complicated design.

Find the bird house on the top shelf. Is the tennis racket **to the left** or **to the right of** the bird house?

'The Bake-a-Cake 3000,' Uncle Vesper announced. 'The machine will cook us delicious cakes in no time. We just need to put all the parts together.' He looked at the others. 'Can you help me?'

Uncle Vesper put the parts on the table. Ember, Nimbus, and the children looked at Vesper's drawing. Then they began to build. They turned the pieces **clockwise** and **anticlockwise**.

Finally, Nadia put the last piece into place.

'I think it's finished!' said Uncle Vesper.

‘Now, move the dial a **quarter turn clockwise** to make the machine work,’ said Uncle Vesper.

Nadia turned the dial. The machine started to rumble.

Has Nadia followed Uncle Vesper’s instructions correctly?

The machine made a loud PING! Warm cakes began to fly out of the machine.

'How do you stop it?' cried Nadia.

'Oh, crumbs! Turn the dial back a **three-quarter turn**!' said Uncle Vesper, catching cake after cake.

Nadia turned the dial to OFF. The machine settled down.

OFF

Nadia has turned the dial back. Is this a **clockwise** or **anticlockwise** turn?

They all enjoyed a wonderful tea party … with lots of freshly made cake. Uncle Vesper and Nini shared stories about their adventures. The children told Nini all about their adventures, too.

When it was time to go, no one wanted to leave.

Uncle Vesper handed the children something small and sparkling. 'Take these back with you,' he said.

'What are they?' asked Nadia.

'They're pieces of a Moon Tail crystal,' explained Uncle Vesper.

Nadia looked at her crystal. It tingled in her hand.

'Moon Tail crystals are special,' said Uncle Vesper. 'When you hold them, you can speak to whoever is holding the other piece of the crystal.' He gave two more pieces to Ember and Nimbus.

'Thank you, Uncle Vesper!' said Nadia.

Nadia couldn't stop smiling. She liked the idea of being able to talk to Ember and Nimbus whenever she wanted to.

She kept the crystal close to her the whole ride back.

Look at the birds. Are they flying **above** or **below** the dragons?

Later, as she curled up in bed, Nadia clutched the crystal tightly.

'Good night, Ember,' she whispered.

From far away, in another world, Ember's voice came back.

'See you soon, Nadia!'

Nimbus's moves

Nimbus loves to fly! Match the correct description to each move.

Nimbus has turned a **quarter turn clockwise.**	Nimbus has turned a **full turn anticlockwise.**	Nimbus has turned a **half turn clockwise.**

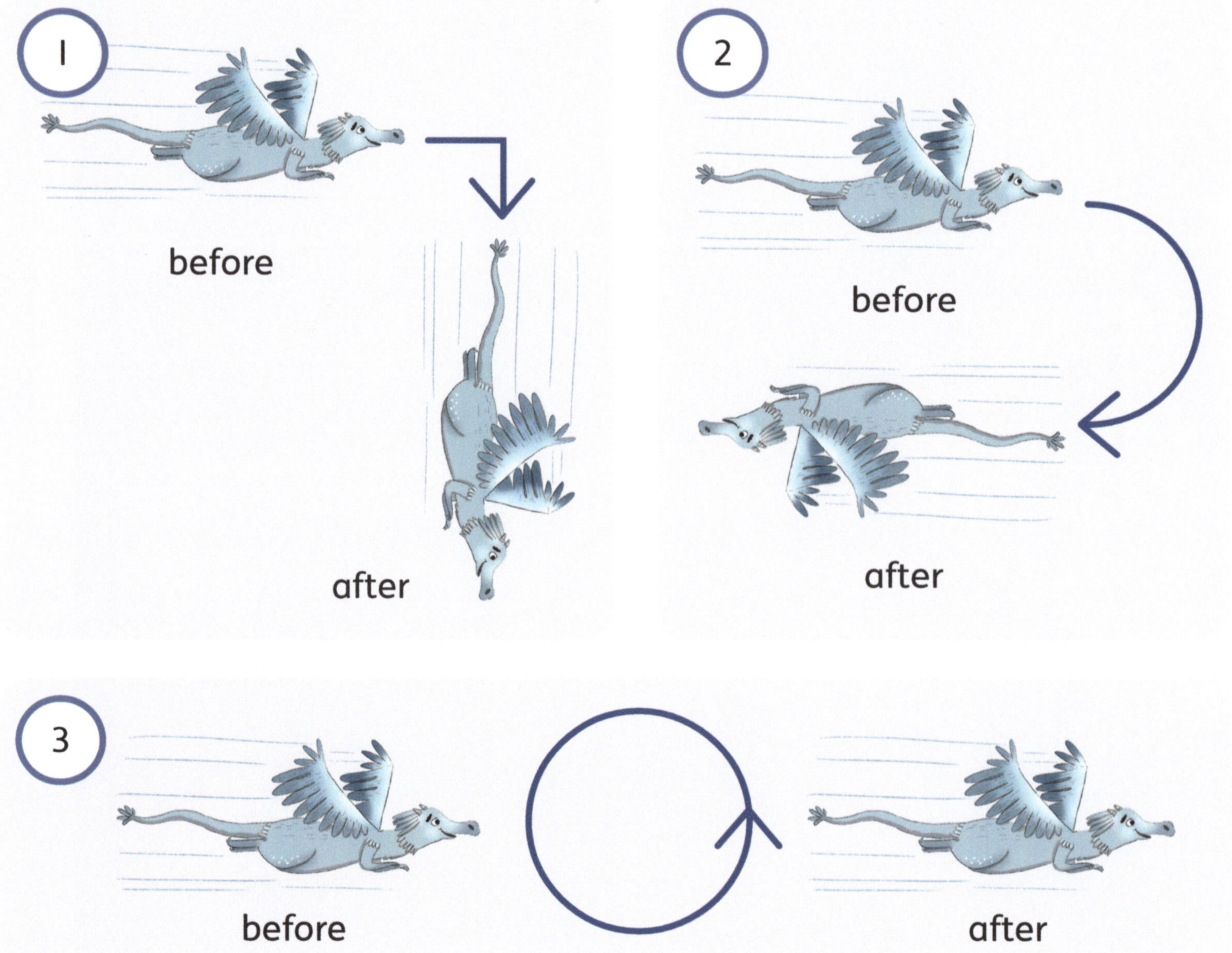

Answers

p4. yes; p5. the opposite direction from where you started; p7. To the right there is the volcano and the lake; p10. Nadia; p13. Nadia; p14. The tennis racket is to the left of the bird house; p17. No, she has turned the dial a three-quarter turn clockwise; p18. anticlockwise; p22. below; p24. 1. a quarter turn clockwise, 2. a half turn clockwise, 3. a full turn anticlockwise.